Alan Brownjohn

LUDBROOKE
AND OTHERS

ENITHARMON PRESS

First published in 2010
by Enitharmon Press
26B Caversham Road
London NW5 2DU

www.enitharmon.co.uk

Distributed in the UK by
Central Books
99 Wallis Road
London E9 5LN

Distributed in the USA and Canada
by Dufour Editions Inc.
PO Box 7, Chester Springs
PA 19425, USA

ISBN: 978-1-904634-96-6

Enitharmon Press gratefully acknowledges the financial support of
Arts Council England, London.

British Library Cataloguing-in-Publication Data.
A catalogue record for this book is available
from the British Library.

Designed in Albertina by Libanus Press
and printed in England by
Antony Rowe Ltd

ALAN BROWNJOHN, whose third volume of *Collected Poems* was published by Enitharmon Press in 2006, was born in 1931. He was educated at Merton College, Oxford. Earlier volumes of verse include *A Night in the Gazebo* (1980), a Poetry Book Society Choice, *The Cat Without E-Mail* (2001) and *The Men Around Her Bed* (2004). He is also a novelist: his fourth novel, *Windows on the Moon* (Black Spring), appeared in 2009. He works as a freelance journalist and critic and lives in London.

ACKNOWLEDGEMENTS

Acknowledgments are due to the following, where most of these poems, or slightly different versions of them, originally appeared: *Acumen*, *Ambit*, *bowwowshop*, *Earl's Court* (Toronto), *The Guardian*, *HQ Quarterly*, *The North*, *Poetry London*, *Poetry Review*, *The Rialto*, the *Spectator*, *Standpoint*, *The Times*, the *Times Literary Supplement* and *Well Versed: Poems from the Morning Star* (edited by John Rety).

A booklet selection of some 'Ludbrooke' poems under the title *Ludbrooke: An Introduction* was published in a limited edition by the Poetry Trust in 2009.

I am grateful to Mr David McCarthy for very kindly informing me at a poetry reading that 'Belisha beacons' (see 'The Beacons, p. 84) in fact only acquired *flashing* lights when black-and-white zebra crossings arrived in the early 1950s. 'December 31st 2009' (p. 108) is contrived in homage to W. H. Auden's '1st September 1939' (see *The English Auden*, edited by Edward Mendelson), the length and form of which it follows.

R. B. Kitaj's *The Caféist* is reproduced on the front cover by kind permission of the painter's estate and Marlborough Fine Art. I am grateful to Marco Livingstone for suggesting the image and to Geoffrey Parton for supplying it electronically.

A.B.

for Steven

CONTENTS

LUDBROOKE

1 HIS MORNING – I

Something rotates his upper half anti-clockwise
Roughly ninety degrees to the left, and his legs overhang
The sanded and polished floorboards he hoped might lift
His morale for a new millennium. Now his eyes,
Which he opens after one or two aerobics,
Can face the wardrobe where twelve laundry hangers
Preserve his dry-cleaned image in a dark cave
The moths have demoted as not worth researching.
An unconscious force has pushed and pulled him outwards
Into another day draining his morale
By a few more drops, if he allows it. He will *not*.
He will take some vigorous action, the simple fact
That he can still stand up makes him optimistic.

2 HIS SEASONAL WISDOM

One should never permit the first perceptible
Shortening of days to suggest that winter
Is a thing to be feared; or show any regret
That the windows have to be closed and locked
Until May at least; or resent the sudden draughts
That stir around one's shoulders – what are *clothes* for
But to wear and be brave in? Puritan aspects
Of Ludbrooke's character give him energy
Towards the end of September. Someone once said
'Ludbrooke shows the resilience of decay.'
His rueful spirit relishes sick leaves
Reeling down, worlds of wanwood, etcetera.
Most fearless creative things are done indoors.

3 HIS 1471

No one has phoned him for what seems several days.
Ludbrooke tries one-four-seven-one, the lonely man's friend,
And confirms it, his last call was on the ninth.
'The caller withheld "their" number.' The adjective 'their'
Annoys the pedantic Ludbrooke, who detects yet another
Example of political correctness. If only
A plural of persons *were* phoning Ludbrooke.
The message suggests it was a commercial call.
The commercial callers hate people to phone back,
People might ring back who hate being targeted.
Sometimes Ludbrooke would love to be targeted
He imagines the short skirt of the targeter walking
Home from the call centre with her mobile off.

4 HIS AUTUMN COURTSHIP

Alma, he says (out-of-date, but her real name,
And who, apart from artistic, nostalgic parents
Would give that to a girl who would reach nineteen
In the twenty-first century?) *Alma, you*
Are interested in music, books and buildings!
Yes, she says, moving her head a little
Away from his approaching beard, though not
In a hurtful way (she is compassionate)
I have destined you, Ludbrooke persists in vain,
For five distinguished intellectual husbands,
Of whom I could be the first and – 'in all modesty –
The least.'

       On this dry day the leaves are scratching
Over Ludbrooke's balcony like small driven bones.

5 HIS NOCTURNE

After about six hours of a challenged daylight
A winter storm finally breaks, its hailstones tin
-tinabulate on the conservatory roof
In the next door garden, where Ludbrooke attended
The local Horticultural Summer Party
At the end of August. Not his thing at all,
They invited him not because he belonged,
Or out of friendship, or out of respect for his status
But as a neighbour to be placated, their having
Hired a cut-price rock group to foster interest
In plants amongst the young. He had picked up Chambers
In search of neglected words to apply to all this,
If he could only refresh them. *Base? Ignominious?*

The exercises continue in his head.
Walk towards me in the mirror, the instructress says.
She walks adroitly backwards as they do that,
Nine clothed individuals, rehabilitating.
Now march on the spot, she insists; and she does it with them.
The mirror is there ten hours later in his bed,
The radio announcing *Minus nine, frost in places*
For when he is asleep.
                          He is still clothed,
But in last month's sheets. Because of the forecast,
He pulls up the blankets. The exercises
Go on even now as he snaps off the bedside lamp
And drifts away through the mirror . . . Forgetting the post-it:
CHANGE THE BEDCLOTHES! To-morrow morning. In
    case she stays.

7 HIS DOG

About young women I was never wrong,
Ludbrooke considers one empty afternoon,
How I have known delectable success
-ive generations of them, followed their fads
From platform shoes to cellphones, was never wrong
When the chips were down and five blouse buttons,
Or a belt and a zip were all that stood between,
Etcetera . . .
        But he has these moments
When the metaphorical hound tugs on its leash
In a bad direction; when an actual dark comes down,
And looks as if it could maul him badly
For his self-deceptions. Times when he stops and asks,
Could I die all the same? Despite all these aerobics?

8 HIS TELECOMS

He believes the phone enables him to talk
To women as he remembers them. Their voices
Haven't changed in years, whereas . . .
'Emma' is pioneer from the Sixties of a popular
Name in the Nineties (how did her parents guess?)
Once he dialled, now he prods at numbers, and –
Hullo, Emma. That is Emma? I thought it was!
Is it convenient to speak? Why I've phoned now
Is because I've remembered something you often said
About being in touch if I felt a black despair . . .
Well I'm seeing this twenty-four-year-old, and
– Hullo? Is that Emma? Is this a bad time – ? I just
So need to talk. Hullo, Emma? Are you there?

9 HIS SCENERY

Visible from his back window in London N.2
Is a said-to-be Chinese knocking-shop; he has seen
A to-ing and fro-ing with some regularity
Of 'slim and elegant' classified-ads girls daily
From early afternoon to late at night.
He won't give it a try.
                              But he does wonder
What on earth could be the Chinese term for
The gentle, purposeful tapping at the door
When the fifteen minutes is up (which, of course,
Gives knocking-shops their name)?
                                          And later thinks
Of a pale pliant hand softly making arrive
Exquisitely and fast a tiny little
Ideogram for that for him for him.

'I got sexual abuse every day when I was a kid.
Every day my father would say, What's that
Little fucker doing now? Reminds me of the one about – about –
[Be aware that this is Ludbrooke's audition] –
'About the two guys who – the two guys who' – [Ludbrooke has
Forgotten the link!] 'the one about the doorbell
Ringing in a brothel' [Ludbrooke's confidence
Returns as he sees they are listening] 'and on the step
Is a man in a wheelchair, no arms, no legs' –
[He remembers to say 'Which isn't funny really'. It gets
A laugh] – and the madam says, Well are you really –
Do you *really* – ? And the guy says, Well . . . I rang the bell, didn't I?'
Thank you, Mr –? Mr Ladbrooke? We'll be in touch.

11 HIS WINTER RECALL

Ludbrooke, much later – or not that much later –
Could kick himself that there was a *Once*
When a chance came, in Alma's winter room
– And he decorously let it pass.
                                        Why, why?
He remembered the following day and the following weeks,
The months and years that followed this lost chance
And carried him on to a *Future* crammed full
With points of *No Return*. Why, why? Except,
Come to think of it, he seized a different chance
On another occasion, he seized it by the arm
And it turned in his direction, it didn't try
To twist away as the first chance might have done.
It became a *Now* with the same despair and pain.

12 HIS DIGITAL

He has been told that 'tuning the radio'
Is acceptable for roughly eighty per cent of women
– For the others the sheer precision is too painful.
Why does Ludbrooke always end up with the others?
With that FM expertise at his finger tips,
Why do so many flinch from it? When
His whole world is available, why draw back?
He fails to see that they are entitled to do that,
Not even escorting his hand to somewhere else.
He fails to see he could try to tune himself
To other manoeuvres, come to that.
Ludbrooke is much entrenched in lazy habit.
Ludbrooke has spent too long never *really* trying.

Posterity punishes women who spurn genius
By confining them to the worst biographers.
If they later try to justify being ungrateful
For the gift fate offered them, it's worse, much worse:
They are condemned to appendices reserved
For persons encountered briefly in internet cafés,
Or met for a moment in Co-op check-out queues.
On the other hand, to comply with Ludbrooke's desires,
And be written for by Ludbrooke, and pointed out
For loving Ludbrooke and winning Ludbrooke's love
– That will have produced an immortality
Almost equal to Ludbrooke's own.
Women, it's Ludbrooke or oblivion!

Ludbrooke desires an honorary degree,
'Desires' being stronger than 'wants' and a euphemism
For 'covets' or 'lusts after'. Is he taking
Ambition to the wire to expect the same honour
As some merely 'famous' crap-merchants like the lead guitar
In 'The Sordid Syndrome'? No, he is not. But the fact
That the lead guitar was doctored should have cancelled his lust
– And it didn't . . . He still wants an honorary degree . . .
Approaching his eighties and undoctored, Ludbrooke
Would accept one from even the New University
Of Leatherhead, for sixty toiling years
At his underpaid vocation.
                                        Ludbrooke suffers
From an MTD: Vanity – a Media-Transmitted Disease.

15 HIS INCONTESTABLE CHARM

He believes it always works. It can be verbal,
– 'We have only met once before, Ms Potterick,
But I remember it so *well* . . .' (Remember 'Ms'
Is part of the ploy. 'Miss' would be wrong and 'Isobel'
Too forward, and banal – Cold Call people call you
By your forename any old dinner time . . .)
                                        Or charm
Can be astutely physical, standing aside
With humorous politeness as the best-looking
Unknown woman enters the party where she and Ludbrooke
Will be trapped with two hours of opportunity
– Or of frustration. She has come with a former
Journalist who traps girls with his former reputation
– And she *leaves* with him!
                        So does it take *more* than charm?

Shows in the delicate way he rests his head
– Despite every fear that she will remove it –
On the shoulder of Miss Chiang to watch *Duck Soup*,
The video, from his reproduction sofa.
The alarm clock rings beside the bed of the man
Made President with the aid of American money
In the shape of Miss Margaret Dumont, and the lovely Miss Chiang
Is completely puzzled by Mr Groucho Marx.
'This gentleman – he is really *President*?' she asks.
Ludbrooke needs to lift his romantic head
To look at her, and answer. As he tries to explain
That this is not quite like life, her mobile rings;
As it does three times on the way back to Finchley Central.

17 HIS CASH FLOW

Varies between a pose of fastidious care
And a pretence of letting it all hang out.
Which to face the world with is a real dilemma,
But he mostly inclines to the first of the two options
As the second might tempt him to leave a wrong impression
Of letting go in every situation,
– Which could be dangerous not to say expensive.
But he does have days of abandon – false abandon –
So that friends might say, 'Whatever you think of Ludbrooke,
He has his own kind of "dash", his own "panache".
To be "devil-may-care" at his age is a talent
Vouchsafed to few, you have to envy him.'
Yes, his friends might say that; though he has yet to
          hear them.

18 HIS STAND-UP – II

He can weather failure, but the thing to do
Is analyse it, take account of it,
Above all keep trying. – Try self-deprecation?
Is it fashionable? Nothing attempted,
Nothing gained is a maxim he has followed for most
Of a gallant life. The group in the vestibule
Outside the studio theatre tries hard to seem
Relaxed, one by one they go in, Ludbrooke is last,
Well-primed with the comedy of failure.
He can't see the panel for the lights. 'Me? At my age?
A stand-up comedian?' he begins. 'As soon as I rose
Someone down there would offer me their seat!'
When the house lights go up he sees three empty chairs.

19 HIS UNIQUENESS

One day he arrives at a sound principle:
What you can't conceal, admit. Make a virtue of it.
Enlist it in your cause. *I shall be unique*
In your experience, he tells the much too
Elegant and slim Miss Chiang, *as your oldest lover,*
More passionate – in proportion to my age –
Than any other man you would ever meet.
She smiles and nods. – But had she understood?
He could not tell, and therefore he could not gauge
The effect of this strategy . . . It would have been
Absorbing, if she had clearly registered
The purpose of his arithmetic, to see
How her culture responded. One more thing never learned.

20 HIS PRIDE

He is not prepared to stand around waiting
For someone to attach the ribbon of the Order
Of the Spare Prick to his soup-stained lapel.
He likes to be noticed, to be the arresting
Centre of an attention he disclaims.
He must never be left alone, and if ignored
When being sociable, he will leave the room
Hoping people will have noticed and say, Well, Ludbrooke
Left pretty early – I wonder why? He knows absence can be
More imposing than presence if done properly.
To-night he has been somewhere just to remind
The buggers that he still exists. Back home early,
In house arrest, he opens the spare bottle.

He believes, at around the eleventh glass
– But really it's just been one continuous glass
Replenished before it's ever emptied,
And that ends the second bottle, *nessa par?* –
He has crossed the boundary from creative
Optimism to embark upon achievement.
He toasts *Achievement!* Possibilities
Come on display now like the endless wares
Of an Istanbul carpet salesman filling up
His tiny cup with coffee, brilliances unrolling
Long vistas ahead of him, happy paths
– That end in colourless nowheres. So . . . the third cork . . .
And the twelfth glass. Lifted to *Relaxed despair.*

Through the office partition he hears someone saying
'Ludbrooke? – A monster!' But of all the big, simple
And final terms of judgement on anyone,
It's about the least offensive. It would give many
More dignity than they deserved to be called 'a monster'
In every legend a monster has been more splendid
Than any human creature dismissable
With one put-down syllable: a monster
Will always breathe more fire than a 'prat' for example,
And clatter more scales than a 'ponce'. In his mirror,
Ludbrooke can easily discern he is not a monster,
He is not disfigured, or frightening, or huge.
– Yet he likes to feel he has the *power* of a monster.

He stops at his local zebra, in front
Of a girl braking her Ford for him radiantly
Visible through her screen of untinted glass.
She has stopped for Ludbrooke alone, he feels favoured
For the first time in weeks, doesn't falter at the kerb,
Strides out with his head turned smilingly towards her,
Puts a kiss on the forefinger and middle finger
Of his right hand, for once an unprepared impulse,
And wafts it to her – and she's smiling back.
A good day, he concludes, as he pushes through
The doors of a supermarket he's ashamed to enter,
And strolls down aisles of plastic groceries thinking,
I can use that kiss again, I really can.

He is dining in an endless restaurant
Three tables away from the Goossens family,
Eugene, Leon, Sidonie. Then Harpo Marx
Comes in, and he sees Sidonie Goossens,
And invites her to go and join him and his brothers
At their own table. 'You're a genuine harpist'
(Yes, Harpo is *speaking*.) 'No thank you,' she says,
I wouldn't want to have a fish or something
Landing in my lap, I'm playing the Wigmore Hall,
Ravel, this evening.'
                    Harpo is there, in the row
Behind Ludbrooke, he listens intently, applauding
With fervour at the end. And then leans over
And asks for Ludbrooke's autograph, if he might?

Revives at the junction of a narrow side street
And the High Street on his journey to the Co-op;
And this time he is the driver: Pedestrians
Pause warily in front of him in case
He lurches forward to join the traffic flow
(Which everybody on wheels would yearn to join)
And one pedestrian is a coutured brunette
Who realises that Ludbrooke is gesturing her
To cross so as to have to a proper look,
A usual ambivalent courtesy. But she does cross,
And she thanks him with a smile that clearly says,
Kind of you, Ludbrooke, I have sussed you out.
Each is quite pleased with this small epiphany.

It snows, and the apprehending officer's
Helmet is, after a minute, a solid
Cake of flakes. But duty is duty, never-
theless. 'If you would be so kind, sir, as to breathe
Into the bag . . .' Ludbrooke smiles and replies
'I only hope that this, whatever the outcome,
Brings you credit in the force. You're a decent bloke
Doing what you are inadequately paid for.'
The peeler pauses, but applies the bag
– And Ludbrooke projects the least far-reaching breath
Since he failed to make it with Gemma – or was it Ruth? –
And issued a short sigh of contempt and shame.
'Next time, sir!' (The darkening constable, on the A12.)

27 HIS COMPLIMENT

A friend says, 'Ludbrooke, you're a conniving sod.'
No smile, no approval or disapproval,
Statement of fact. And he reflects on it
In one of his usual venues of reflection:
The bath, the Co-op check-out queue, in bed
Before he gets up. Yes, he's felt exactly that
For many decades. He knows his instinct for finding
A devious route to any given objective
Other men would approach by motorway,
Breaking down en route. Among the smoking wrecks
Of all their projects he moves with ruthless care
And predatory compassion, grinding small.
Ludbrooke pretends he never grinds at all.

At Tottenham Court Road station (its real name)
He draws back at the top of the escalator
To let the balefully striding young woman
Go first. As they descend, she turns and says,
'That was charming of you!' Ludbrooke replies,
'Oh I like to act the gentleman.' 'But you *are*
A gentleman', she insists. 'Don't tell me it's acting.
Where have you been to-night?' He hesitates,
Then decides to be truthful. 'At a conference.'
'What kind?' 'A business seminar.' Not true.
'Oh', she answers. 'My young brother goes to those.'
Then 'This is mine', she exclaims at a sudden train.
He hesitates again. 'Mine's the next one.' Not true either.

There are not enough anecdotes about him
Coming back to Ludbrooke. 'Ludbrooke, is it true that – ?'
'Are we really to believe – ?' But in his bath
He has two revelations: One that it's possible
His friends are protecting him, that the four walls
Between which scandalous secrets are spread around
Are fortress-like after all, that he has friends
Who like him enough to reinforce them.
– And the second is that charisma can be developed
By letting it be known that you are aware
Of certain displeasing stories which, of course,
Are quite untrue, and merely degrade the teller,
One of Ludbrooke's enemies . . . Two birds with one stone, then.

Ludbrooke remembers saying to a girl
Watch this space! Which girl he can't recollect,
Or the space in which he planned to reappear.
He seems to think it had been a time for action,
A time for trying out some new approach;
But his only action had been to bark *Watch this space!*
And smile, he hoped intriguingly, as he left her
– And was that enough to count as an 'approach'?
Then whether he said it sober or after drinking
He is unsure. He keeps this metaphorical
Cabinet of approaches for future use.
How is it they gather dust even in the darkness
Of metal drawers too cumbersome to pull out?

He does not concede that any quality
Essential if one wants to look civilised
Is actually beyond him. He expects
To be thought well-informed, open-minded, and controlled
In every sort of appetite; hear people say
'It may be an outdated word, but Ludbrooke is *virtuous*.'
Yet somehow . . . He knows that *somehow* is a vague excuse
For his sequences of ignorance, prejudice
Or secret immoderation – another sly term.
With the help of *somehow* he can blame things on time,
Or poor luck, or other people, get off the hooks
Of duty and obligation – even of love –
And still feel virtuous for trying so very hard.

Begins with a dinner of steamed vegetables,
Arranged round a fishcake eaten to mark
The Reduced Price sell-by-date on which
It went into his freezer one month before.
It's a Saturday, he could leave the washing-up,
But when he returns to his chair he has done it all,
Stacked it up in the kitchen cabinet, slammed the door,
And resorted again to his lengthening pencil list
Of the ways of restructuring a muddled life.
One is this: to consider four files retrieved
From a 'dedicated' drawer, three dating back
A year or two, the fourth new – and slim; and promising.
He sips a brew of resented herbal tea.

Concludes with this fourth file; preserving the one card
That came in response to three nervous letters,
And ending with the word they had agreed
Might finish a loving message in her own language.
But since he can't clearly read what preceded it,
He can't tell if it's sincere, or a joke sent
In whimsical recall of their single meeting
On that train long halted in a mountain tunnel.
They were alone in the eight-seat compartment.
They smiled. Ludbrooke courteously opened
His bottle of star-fruit liqueur, the national drink,
And they shared a few sips from its cap . . . Now he goes
To the kitchen for a tumbler, and drains the rest.

Have included Luciana (foreign for 'Lucy'),
Tempted out on a cloudy summer day
To a different cafeteria. Ludbrooke, buying
The coffee – and the croissant – or the sandwich –
Tries (in her language) to get her to compare it
With the one where she works. It's her day off,
And he calls this 'your semi-liberation'. She smiles
As he tries to find a favourable moment
For suggesting they go back to his flat,
And make this a 'wholly liberated' day
Relaxing on his balcony, hearing him speak
Her language badly with an English charm
– Until, he hopes, the rain drives them indoors.

'I am only marginally acquainted with
The niceties of the latest colloquial English',
Says the very newest illegal immigrant
Into Ludbrooke's settled life. 'What you need', he replies,
'Is practice with someone whose entire passion is language
In all its subtle variousness.' She understands.
'A regular dialogue', he goes on, 'with someone cognisant
Of the ways in which English changes from year to year.
Someone discerning and relishing the process . . .'
'So how could I meet such an individual?'
She asks him, still without any suspicion.
'I don't know,' he shrugs. 'But I feel it is essential.
The next time we meet I might have a suggestion.'

On one occasion he has cooked rather well,
And she's actually eaten most of it for once.
There's a silence requiring something to be said
– Or done, perhaps? He takes up her free hand
And, having tried this on himself, applies
The dried-with-his-upper-front-teeth tip of his tongue
Very delicately to the narrow gap between
The long nail and the skin of her middle finger,
While she sits and watches him, bemusedly.
This Ludbrooke gesture receives its première between
His main course of monkfish and his option
Of fresh fruit – or biscuits and mild cheddar.
When she takes back the tested finger and extends its hand
To a peach in his bowl, it's still too close to call.

This is my bedroom, he says in a casual voice,
And lo, my bed, below my photograph
Of the Acropolis. (*My love-making*, he thinks,
And sometimes even dares to say all this out loud
Is like the Acropolis, an edifice
Wonderful to have experienced even once,
And transformative *to have known for a little longer.*
Sufficient of the Acropolis remains
In its incomparable magnificence
To stir a sensitive girl for years to come.
Those who forego it weep at what they have missed
When their chance has vanished. And then he adds
Intelligent girls adore *the Acropolis.*)

He becomes aware that it might not be much fun
To be his latest, *the one he really loves*
– His italics, in his e-mail she reads at work.
He recycles the thought in the message he leaves
When he calls her at home that evening, and she is out.
Her cold-voiced message ends, and the promised bleep
Is heard after several seconds, and he begins:
'You must know you are the one I've really *loved*,
And I'm quite aware of how difficult that must be . . .'
Trailing off in all false modesty. He has a phone
That gives out a wail when he replaces it,
As he does now, on its 'base unit'. He looks at it.
He thinks, 'When I try tactics I know I'm losing.'

He can do nothing right. Should he blame himself?
His gifts are received without the least pretence
Of surprise or gratitude. The 'kids' cry at his jokes
And confirm he was right not to think of them as 'children'.
The gate bangs in the night, Ludbrooke left it open.
His latest introduces him to male friends
Whom he cannot assess, but assumes are devious bastards.
The cat spits at Ludbrooke, who has sent ahead
A reputation for being good with cats.
He tried to help with the meal but is dissuaded.
He hates lace counterpanes, and he has one,
On which his pen leaks. Should he blame himself for all this?
He should not. He just attracts appalling hosts.

Should his latest always supersede his previous
With the speed of a cut in a film to a daylight scene
After an unresolved darkness? – A busy street,
A nearby table in a pavement café,
Small redhead alone with a sandwich, empty days
In the diary pages she turns forward – back – forward – back.
Let me settle this, five minutes after she lets him join her.
No , you mustn't. You re-a-lly mustn't . . . Oh well, then.
He enquires about a next meeting. *I can't this week,*
Next, possibly . . . Freedom and dignity safeguarded.
A young bald man passes, turns back, kisses
Ludbrooke's latest on the cheek. *Who's he? – Oh – him!*
Mr Ridyard – Creativity Consultant.

He has noted in a long lifetime that many friends
Have lapsed into partnerships that do not meet
Their early expectations, but served, endured,
Delivered mortgages. Too late for that,
Time only for the particular panache
At which he excels, like paying that place in Swansea
To buy her initials for his car number plate
– Or naming a main course she says she likes
After her. *Yes, there are some recipes*
We remember because a famous chef or other
Dreamed them up. But the truly immortal dishes
Are those conceived by great sculptors, poets, composers,
Novelists, painters. He will recall one soon.

Ludbrooke doesn't practise jealousy. He
Has perfected it, deconstructed it, and junked it.
Impersonal tolerance rules. *Let them flirt*
With whomever they like, I am indifferent.
– Olympian, he waits for his latest to return
To his side at a particularly nasty party.
But she doesn't return.
                    He looks for her and finds her.
She moves away smiling, as if she hasn't seen him.
She is small, and very beautiful.
Ludbrooke is tall but he can't make out whether
She is still in the room. *Is she still in the* bloody *room?*
Is her anorak still on the hook in our hostess's hall?
– Nothing like jealousy for making you feel younger.

He would like to have done what the man did in the film,
When he left the woman's flat and went downstairs,
Then suddenly turned and tiptoed up again
And 'pressed his ear to the door' for twenty minutes,
Being able to hear all they said after he had gone
– Then finally, with footsteps audible inside,
Stayed in that same position as the door opened
And was discovered lurking but not embarrassed.
The man in the film just stood there guiltlessly smiling,
While the eavesdropped couple gasped and stared at him
With the certainty he had heard what he should not have.
He would like to have done it like the man in the film,
But it needed boldness, luck, and a thin door.

Ludbrooke is tall but cannot wish he was
The moderate size of Ridyard, a smaller man
Who seems to attract simultaneous pity and desire
From tall strong girls. He suspects that man with his latest.
She takes a small-scale sort of feminine beauty
Past the point where he can describe it, and on
To the verge of perfection. It's any movement she makes . . .
She has only to turn towards him with her ambivalent
Half-smile for him to gaze down, he imagines,
As at a locket painted for someone to carry
To some Peninsular War or other and maintain
His loyalty; never tested, then, by what buzzes
In her handbag now. That's *Ridyard's* ringtone . . .

You can turn a stone and see things run away
From the sudden enlightenment of their grimy patch.
And you flinch, and you loathe, and at the same time pity:
Look, this one is injured, poor thing, it can't run
As fast as the others, its years of self-infliction
Have encouraged others to inflict on it as well.
Those others are now scurrying to adapt
To the dangerous nature of the light, already
Reorganizing their patch as a passable
Adaptation to the truth. Found out, they have to pretend
They were always environmentally spotless
– Which the injured insect finds difficult.
Such is Ridyard. Such is Ridyard's agency.

It was only plentiful in Ridyard's childhood.
In his adolescence it fell across his forehead
As if it could only just hang on to his scalp.
In his twenties it did an untactical retreat
In the opposite direction, all his efforts
Were given to fetching it forward again. He stopped
Trying that at about thirty-one, he bunched what remained
Above and behind his ears like last redoubts
– Inglorious failures, always. Then, one day,
He shaved himself to a baldness he pretended
Was the fashion and entirely his own choice.
Under bare ice-caps and deserts there sometimes lurk
Resources worth exploring. In this case, not.

There is a group photograph with Ridyard
Egregious in it, projecting himself as if
There were no to-morrow, in the front row leering,
With Ludbrooke somehow elbowed to the back.
His latest's arm is round Ridyard, that's quite clear,
And she smiles as she does that for the picture,
It's OK for a photograph. Isn't it?
Ludbrooke now takes the nearest implement, nail scissors,
And cuts out her smiling face to keep
(In his wallet, maybe?) And, released from Ridyard,
She is beautiful again. But there's something else
That he spots later on: it's a forced and fraudulent smile.
It's in his wallet, an ambiguous comfort.

48 HIS RESOLUTION

He settles down to get the Ridyard problem
Into perspective, granted Ridyard *is* a problem:
Sometimes he seems not one man but all mankind,
Or any of it pursuing Ludbrooke's latest.
He might be wilfully ugly and unprepossessing,
Or, ostensibly at least, polite and decent.
He might have more talent than Ludbrooke, or maybe not
(His latest's judgement might not be accurate)
He might have so many faces you couldn't count them.
– So here's Ludbrooke's resolution: to discount any man
Impinging on his latest in his thoughts,
While hoping he impinges on her in *their* thoughts.
Swings and roundabouts. He can sleep now. Or he can't.

One evening his very latest has 'some sad news'
(If this is sad, what is hilarious?)
Ridyard failed to impress with a 'presentation'
And was 'surplus to requirements' the same afternoon.
Ludbrooke never practises *schadenfreude* of course . . .
Even the least attractive sort of post-modern creature
Deserves a passing compassion; especially if
He can advance his cause by showing it.
It's a disgraceful world, he says, happy to appear
To console, although he is not applying
'Disgraceful' to what has happened, but to Ridyard's world.
It surprises and impresses her when his hand
Closes briefly over hers. *I'm sorry . . .You liked him?*

One day he recalls being thirteen in the mire
Of the Second World War; when they nevertheless
Found the time, skill and means to repair his ankle, fractured
On the Recreation Ground roundabout. He knew
There was space enough for friends and classmates to follow
The usual custom, and he greatly looked forward
To collecting their names and their jokes on his ample plaster
– But nobody offered . . . Nobody at all . . .
He remembers the feeling, and smarts – as they say –
At the ostracism implied; though very soon after
He was subtly spreading round various other ideas:
That it wasn't his style; that they held him in too much awe;
That he shone with too much charisma, even then.

She continues to sit there scowling in his memory
With her hands on her head, Mr Campbell's punishment
For anyone shouting out something in class
– And it was all his fault. He had pretended to find
Her name in his birthday present dictionary,
And he read out a meaning he made up there and then:
'A ferocious tiger found in tropical forests.'
She exploded. 'What? Me?' He was nine years old,
So was she, Mr Campbell was forty-six
('Campbell: a prehistoric schoolteacher').
Ludbrooke was not ashamed at his trick. He was proud.
He was sorry for the girl; but she forgave him,
The first to acknowledge his inventiveness and wit.

And one day there turns up Pettiford, a man
In his fifth form fifty years before
But not seen since – until this chance meeting and drink
On Waterloo Station. Pettiford still has
The same merry look, but the smile has hardened.
So was his schoolboy grin mere ingratiation?
Pettiford has come to see all human dealings
– Including love affairs – as 'marketing'.
He says, 'If you like call me "neo-liberal"'.
Ludbrooke concludes that time is far less crucial
Than some inherent gene guaranteeing ambition . . .
He tries, ambitiously, to market himself next day
To his shaving mirror. Is he really selling *that*?

Good news for his friends? After two miles, about,
On a cardiac treadmill, his body plastered
With terminals gauging his durability,
A report spools out of a computer (once
He despised computers) to the effect
That the chances of his living another five years
Are ninety-five per cent. He steps down, walks out
Into an ambiguous daylight of lesser ailments:
Are his knees quite right? Does the jolting of the bus
Mean his kidneys require attention? Are there supposed
To be jagged blurs on the mobile ads in the street,
Or is this a migraine? In view of all this, he asks
Just *what* remains for me now? – Well, success, for a start.

He puts on his brightest suit in gratitude
For a morning of provisional sunshine. He shops,
He takes a coffee among the no-hopers in
The franchised cafeteria of the Library.
When it's lunch time (this is summer) the Girls' School
Seniors come out for a drag ('Look out for Miss Pender!')
In the High Road a giggle announces something.
'Excuse me – Emily thinks you're someone *famous*.
Is it true?' 'Well, my name is Ludbrooke,' he says,
Half-flattered and half-embarrassed. 'Emily,'
His interlocutress calls, 'You heard of *Ludbrooke?*'
But she has gone . . . Besides, the one who asked
Is his opportunity; or so he thinks.

But the next day he goes out at the same time
And Christ, it's raining, no Seniors, no Emily,
No mandated representative to approach him!
It seems the whole Girls' School has put on winter wear
Against the dismal drop in temperature.
He reverts to the Library and Schopenhauer.
But he does take a break for a lonely sandwich in
Their bland cafeteria at ten past one.
A meticulous history mistress, having marked
That morning's essays, takes a sandwich too.
She is fortyish and looks approachable,
And after the second smile he goes across.
'I'm Ludbrooke,' he says. And she, 'I'm Libby Pender.'

Ludbrooke also is meticulous, a 'Gentleman
Of the Week-at-a-View Desk Diary'
Would be his role and title, were there such.
He has in fact noticed Ms Pender driving off
At three fifty-five exactly, the departure of
A commuter from far out avoiding the traffic.
In her rear window 'The ———— don Garden Club'
Is not him at all. 'Libby Pender'
Does cross her legs rather well, but with just the lunch hour . . .
In a week he would be buying her lunch, for what?
There are other plans, surely, with which to fill
His workless, playless, friendless blank pages.
They finish their sandwiches and it goes no further.

Always too knackered to remember what he packed
And the suitcase he used, he stands at the carousel letting
Some bizarre unwieldy thing go past
Three times before he says, *Sod it – that one's mine!*
He has finally seen the label to be his own,
Its illegible scrawl, its origin in
A travel agency bankrupt some months past;
And he has to stand and wait now for its fourth circuit,
Coming back by itself as if all the bags around it
Had shrunk away in immaculate disgust.
In his dream that night, all the travellers waiting with him
Are young women cramped with convulsive, unpleasant laughter
When he lunges to grab at this symbol of himself.

He books into a half-a-star hotel
In a non-cathedral city. Her mobile is off.
Whose mobile? He goes to their once-favourite
Restaurant where he half expected to dine her.
She does not show up. And this place only serves wine
By the bottle. So, never mind, he'll take
What he doesn't manage back to his hotel room
– Except he won't, the waitress has binned the cork
And pours constant fill-ups, soon he's drunk the lot.
The evening, like many others, away or home,
Is a stuporous failure, it founders in a mire
Of unworthy effort. But can he say, *Serve me right?*
No, he can't. (Whose mobile? His latest-before-last's.)

When he checks out, the man who takes his laundry
Is at Reception sorting out bills and receipts.
He is man of cultural refinement
Who can summon up a disarming turn of phrase:
'I see we're still washing your Oxfam shirt, sir.
It has seen better days – few of them with you.'
It occurs to Ludbrooke that if, like any other
Civilised man, he keeps a graded list
Of his larger garments (stopping short of what
The hotel calls 'private items') and changes one when
It falls below C+, he should listen
To this man regarding this shirt, which he now wears
To go home in, having awarded it a B.

His walk to the kitchen is an act of valour
That few could manage with the same *aplomb*
– Or so he tells himself with an outdated noun
From boys' adventure stories, where among those
Who possess it is the wounded scout not flinching
Before the surgeon, the leader who knows what to do
In the jungle ambush, the School cricket captain
No one guessed was the heir to a Balkan throne.
– Though it could be applied to a scoundrel: 'With insolent
Aplomb he picked up the duelling pistol.' Ludbrooke
Would accept any role that gave him what he finds
In Chambers' Dictionary after his lemon tea:
'Perpendicularity, self-possession, coolness.'

...AND OTHERS

AND THIS IS ME

1

In the kitchen, seen from behind through
the open 'lounge' door thinking, Out here
almost everything could have a post-it saying
Speed me into a more useful future please,
via the bin, the black sack and the boot,
the one-way drive to my next destination,
its rough but genial welcome, its widening acres.
How good of my clapped-out camera to wait
ten seconds before flashing its final
cameo of my home life: making a list
of everything I hate that's reusable,
that or for melting down. Should I also take
my donor card for the Paper Only?

2

– Going up the green metal steps
at the Recycling Centre of the borough.
From the top there's a remarkable view
of a deep lasagne of cardboard, to which I'm adding
boxes flattened at the request of the Council.
To my left, you can just see it, over there,
is another geology, a profoundly dedicated
skip of junked computers. Should I have brought
bit by bit my entire household, Hitachi
Samsung, Zanussi, Applemac?
And my wardrobe contents? . . . I don't like
the receptacle (not in my viewfinder here)
where they take whatever you have worn:
shoes, socks, pants, trousers, blouses,
your body having gone on to another place.

3

– And this is me on the day I left at last,
by the glass case filling with small sharp implements,
a tangle of penknives, scissors, fountain pens,
a teddy bear with horrid plastic claws.
This one was taken against the rules, when the private
heavies were all preoccupied uncapping
inhalers, confiscating hair grips, passing cameras
like my new one, which went a moment later
along the x-ray belt, its film surviving,
as witness these holiday snaps.
And why should I have *liked*
the quasi-medical touching that confirmed
I had no excrescence requiring them to detain me?
That my Brent Cross braces contained no cartridges?
That proved my sandals were for walking and not exploding?
That my clothes were empty of everything
except myself and the chip I was becoming?

MY CRICKET

Began with watching war-stricken soldiers play
At a military hospital where I – if you please! –
Was a guinea-pig patient having his blood replaced
As a possible cure for childhood allergies.
On a makeshift wicket in the grounds, on a calm day
Of collateral sunshine, Wilson faced
Deliveries from Todd, with Baxter his runner ready
– And blocked ball after ball. Down in the book
Went platoons of diagonal pen-strokes, filling
Neat box after box – until that sudden hook,
Wilson's only stroke, dispatched his steady
Partner with bat thrust forward, willing
His own lame leg to win them a safe run.
When he'd reached the crease, Wilson would join him there,
Hobbling slowly down to wait for his next chance,
Which would come without warning as soon as one
Loose ball in about four overs provided a fair
Opportunity for scoring. From his grim trance
Of concentration, Wilson would suddenly
Emerge, open his shoulders – and eight – nine – ten
Came up in slammed singles made when he'd seen a gap
In the legside field, Baxter judging exactly when
He should start to lurch forward doggedly
Down the uneven pitch. Those two could wrap
A game up one run at a time, achieving
Through sheer persistence what other men would try
To accomplish by risk and daring and get nowhere.
Sixty-six years on I remember them, and lie
Awake in the blacked-out ward, with bombers leaving
Overhead for Cologne, and still can't bear
To imagine their futures. I myself left half-cured

Of my ailments by rigorous exercise with their drill-
Sergeant in the gym, which I had to attend
For my own rehabilitation. Did their firm will
Mean they recovered strength enough to be assured
Of more horrors, in desert or jungle? Or in the end,
Did they simply limp away, declared exempt
From extra bloodshed, to die in saner places?
I've tried in vain to work out how some can let
Life's harsh deliveries hurtle towards their faces,
And either ignore them, or clobber them with contempt.

Some things you never learn but can't forget.

ORPHEUS IN THE METRO

The story is he looked round at Eurydice
And lost her because he looked.

But it isn't true, he didn't look at her,
He turned his back and with his free hand found

Eurydice's somehow in the pell-mell carriage
And held on to it until they had to move

To an opening door, and pulled her through the gap
Before it closed to carry them away.

Then he walked with her side by side up the long stairs
Not looking even then, until at the top

He finally did turn when it was daylight,
And they were free to look face to face and smile

On the bridge over the highway
At Coyuya.

                              (Ciudad de Mexico)

PRECISELY

On 'All Souls' Night' (well, Yeats used the idea,
And I'll use it, atheistic though I am)
I sit and slurp the best blended I can find
For £9.99 ('Produce of Scotland', 'Selected
For the Co-operative Group'), having pulled the curtains
And turned out the lamps all over NW3.
It's about four hours since the laser precision
Of Mr Staghurst-Jones (his real name? No)
Was applied to the retina of my ailing eye,
Which had constantly preferred to deliver me,
For about six months, any horizontal line
With blurs and undulations; a malicious trick
To play on one addicted to what the world describes
As a 'recreation' to rank with 'hill-walking'
Or 'angling' – i.e., 'reading.'
                                    Now it's five-forty,
And with a thudding headache, the natural
Aftermath of the expertise I was afforded
By Mr Staghurst-Jones, with low murmurs
To his team (too low for my muffled ears),
With the headache stopped by aspirin and Arden House,
This solid eye-patch replaces it as my fear.
It's been put on to protect me, but wearing it
I can't tell if Mr Staghurst-Jones succeeded
Or failed, as the case may be . . .
                                    In his preamble,
In the low-key high-tech consulting room, he had
By law to tell me whatever might accrue
Or just follow from this procedure: There might be
'Improvement, no alteration, haemorrhage,
Detachment, or loss of vision. Only one or two per cent
Lose the sight of the eye.' I sighed and thanked him
In anticipation – 'Always encourage!'

Was also used by Yeats.
                                    Against the dark
I raise another slurp: 'To state-of-the-art
Ophthalmic surgery – and Mr Staghurst-Jones!'
Do I think I can hear the pushing-back of chairs
As they all stand to life their glasses, those long tables
Of eyeless skeletons wishing me luck
When the patch comes off at precisely ten to-morrow?

ODE TO INSOMNIA

You are the queen of opportunities, the chance
To stumble and grope in refrigerated light
For the crust of sliced wholemeal in a plastic wrap,
And spread it with honey to finish in the dark
– Or to answer a letter with a purposeful
Clarity daytime would hedge and qualify.

– Or just to take up the headphone offer
Of *Turandot* or whatever . . . Don't believe
I worship you with despairing twists and turns,
I come to you straight. And when worship falters,
It's with waves on endless beaches, or the rotation
Of cakes in a somewhere strip-lit cavern of glass.

ON A BIRTHDAY

Summer night fallen, and the light outside
Exchanged for a reflection of ourselves
In the café glass, the tannoy playing
Soave sia il vento in the room adjoining
The bakery where earlier they made
The cake on which the candles couldn't be
Lighted because of a somewhere draught from
An open door soon shut to oblige us
– Then the baker's thumb flicked hard on the wheel
Of the lighter again, again, again;
But flames at last so I could blow with closed
Eyes as they swayed and flattened to die out
(And keep my hope to myself.) Then you said
'You can open them', and I did and saw
The threads of smoke that rose across your smile
As you sang with our reflections smiling
In the July dark, one mile from the dome
Through which we had seen, as they meant us to,
The sky, this day being one week only
Short of an anniversary I'll have
To try to reconcile with a happiness.

(Hiroshima 28/7, Café Mozart)

THE BEACONS

Am I hearing them in the dark, reliving the daylight
Of seventy years ago? Her cries of fright
For my safety, in her dread of what she might

See next? Am I feeling now her fury when I made
The opposite kerb untouched? I should have stayed
Till she beckoned me across, but I disobeyed,

Ran out between the studs, saw my face
Staring out at me from a polished space
That brushed my buttons but left no instant trace

On the child inside the blazer, and sped off fast
On its own careless venture.
                          For the last
Ten silent minutes I have seen my past

From to-night's bedroom window, watched the beacons flash
At the crossing below, remembered a childhood dash
Which could have proved fatal; resembling my rash

Return to the drink-shelf in a room filled
With the lifelong effects of my not then getting killed,
As if something contradictory in me willed

Both the danger and the safety? Well, I'm still alive . . .
(And the beacons? Hore-Belisha's, who would survive
To lose his seat in nineteen forty-five.)

A MODERATE NIGHTMARE

In one of my moderate nightmares I have
The perfect booking, arrive in good time at the station,
My window-seat clean, its upholstery old-fashioned,
The prospect from the look of my few fellow-passengers,
Boding well for the journey; but the train stands still.
It's motionless for hour after hour after hour,
On each side only the windows of two other trains
Completely unlighted and empty, it's dark outside
And no hope of starting to-night.
                                        But then,
An Announcement: the ground will soon start moving,
And Oxford will be arriving at Paddington
In just under two hours. In my scholarship suitcase
On the rack above, my clock starts going round backwards
To when the alarm rings reminding me
It's time to pack it so my bed can make itself
While I dress up ready for my solemn walk
Through the parted crowd outside the station
Where I am headed, each big step nearer
Achieving the hungry aspirations
Of my adolescence, which I suddenly realise
(With a dark doubt of all my purposes)
Began as far back as the different colours which graded
The tiny spellings on Miss Palmer's postcards
When I was five, and in the infants' class
– The day of my earliest misreadings.

THE DUST

The silence was different because the sounds
Before it had been different. It grew deeper
With every new bend in the upward road
Through the parched mountain forest; until

I began to hear, where the track steepened,
Turned suddenly uphill and straightened out,
Sounds entering my ears from higher still,
Something bearing down on me from above,

Checking speed by braking on bend after bend,
Coming nearer with every step of my threatened life
On this upward venture into more and more dust,
On a stony track in another hottest summer.

Then the truck arrived with its grey bridal train of dust
On the straight itself, ten seconds up ahead.
I stood still on the only ledge above
A deep green drop that might have checked a fall,

And raised a hand, smiling, to a windscreen where
Another hand raised itself, someone smiling back
Acknowledging me, and leaving me again
Looking down alone through a settling cloud

At the shuddering cargo of logs that had been trees,
Each longer than the length of the truck itself;
At the end of the very largest, no white- or red-
Or any-coloured rag to warn about what it carried.

THE GRAVITY

now he is going to
fall and his hand goes out to
a fence but he wrenches the
whole thing out of
the ground and he staggers and
grabs at a post which
collapses and carries him
over the bank of
the river he hadn't
noticed was there, its
dry mud verge is almost as
hard as any stone for
falling on and he might
have gone over but for the
fence and the post and his stag-
gering in the hope he
would regain his balance and
not be destined as soon as
this to go down with
the gravity with the gravity

SHIFTS

No one else at the steam outlet,
She's down on her lucky pavement
Near the end of the snoutcast wall
Outside the hospital, holding
A can that spills each time she lifts it
Tremblingly towards her lips.
She shifts her weight for a second,
One cheek to the other cheek on
The stone slab, and begins to sing
'Here comes the sun . . .' They ignore her,
Breathe in, exhale and murmur. In
Someone's overall pocket a phone
Rings – with greener grass at the end
Of the line? Not really, her mother again,
She ignores it.
              '"You've got to make shift
To be happy," I've told her, "but not
With a widower of eighty."
When it comes to your own mother
You have to speak your mind.' Good advice,
The trampwoman thinks, and drinks up.
A sunlight suddenly favours
The length of the wall, and she rests
The emptied can on the pavement
With care, then shifts her cheeks again
In a rush of warmth from the vent.

Eight 'Of' Poems

OF AN ESCALATOR

Oh it's dawn after winter dawn to be carried down
Past the jiggling panels to the corridors,
And through NO ENTRY (always a short cut)

And out to the point on the platform where the door
Invariably opens, and he's inside wanting to scream,
Which no one would heed, though they're wanting to scream
                                themselves.

One Friday the moving steps and his card
Deliver him up and into the dark to an Ice
Palace. Outside it, in polar moonlight, a man

In a red robe fumbles in a sack for his reward.

OF A DILEMMA

Going home on the Northern Line having had too much,
I sense, for once, a sociable atmosphere,
No frowning at micro-screens, no paranoid staring.

Should I speak to the similarly binge-drunk girls
Smiling at me in all bare-legged innocence?
I smile back, but speak to none of them, picture of

(I consider) a most gentlemanly reserve.
– And I could have spoken, we spent ten minutes halted
Between Camden Town and Chalk Farm, and the world for once

Seemed tolerant of tie-wearing patrician elders.

OF A FINANCIAL SCANDAL

It hit the fan at approximately eight-fifteen,
On a day in that terrible October,
And sprayed all over the latest *haute couture*

– Which was seen, when the screams died down, to have survived.
All the talk initially was about the dreadful s.
Bu the s. was soon forgotten.
                                    And the fan slowed down

Until its individual blades could be seen
Going round with solid confidence. So the talk
Reverted to all the old topics, a voice remarking,

See, it's stopped altogether, now it's all right again.

OF AN AIRMAN'S UNDERSTATEMENT

For some it could be the desert heat, for others
Monsoon rains. But the very worst of all,
Remembered all of fifty-seven years afterwards?

– 'The unbelievable cold in the fuselage
In the "stratosphere" from which we had started bombing.
I felt for Grant . . . He had to relieve himself,

And his urine froze. And his – well, he himself
Froze to the metal can. I can't hear the phrase
"I couldn't tear myself away" without being

Twenty-six thousand feet above firestorm Dresden'.

OF THE LITTLE HEADS

It was one thing to have the car door opened
So he could step out into the daily crowd;
And one thing to have the heads around his neck

Blue purple yellow black soft and deferential,
Bestowing importance on each chosen word
– And another to wake up one morning and find them gone,

His perpetual necklace scattered invisibly
Over the colourless ground of a world
Where he drove all the way by himself, switched off

And stepped out alone again. Alone into no one.

OF A CASE OF AUTHORITY

You can tell the woman in charge by the keys at her waist
And her abruptness straightening all the chairs.
At the end of the day before she locks the doors.

This is the end of the pier, where Tina wanted
Les Six on the tannoy, she brought her own CD,
But also where Management switched it off at once,

And we were left with a silence before Abba
(Admittedly a very pure sort of silence).
So how can a beautiful woman with keys on her belt

Despoil her beauty by turning off Tailleferre?

OF AN OFFER

An hour and a quarter, and only a mile from the airport . . .
Probably two more hours to the Centre, so
We have reached an agreement about the new President,

We have chastised the national captain of Track Events,
We are getting on fine. Then suddenly in this tailback,
The taxi-man offers to show me scenes of himself

In flagrante with his girl-friend. On his mobile. I decline,
I can picture the sort of thing. – But I do not wish
To hurt his feelings. I say, 'Do forgive me, the glasses

I require for any close work are still in my suitcase.'

OF A REQUIREMENT

There came a voice intoning compliments:
'You have led – how shall I say? – a *magnanimous* life,
Been self-effacing, generous and strong.

So you will be rewarded, despite the fact
That reward was never your object in behaving
In the principled fashion you have. There remains

Only one thing you must do. To comply
With the customary procedures, please click on
And follow the links, and – where requested – enter

The invoice for your fee plus any expenses'.

DRINKING SONG

I heard a lonely man in a bar
Sing *Here's to animals!*
– Unwittingly toasting every she
In a nearby Girls' Academy.
(Chorus of Professors:)
      If he had felt any tremor of doubt
      He could have left some of our students out,
      Not all are perfect. But he didn't.
      So – all together now – *Here's to animals!*

I heard a hungry man in a bar
Sing *Here's to vegetables!*
– Unknowingly praising every root
Or stalk or bough that provided fruit.
(Chorus of Ecologists:)
      If he'd been liable to pick and choose,
      He would have been content to lose
      A few examples. But he wasn't.
      All together now – *Here's to vegetables!*

I heard a sturdy man in a bar
Sing *Here's to minerals!*
– Rejoicing in all the age-long stayers,
Alps and Andes and Himalayas.
(Chorus of Geologists:)
      If he hadn't adored every rock and stone
      He should have left some of them alone,
      They're hazardous. But he couldn't.
      All together then, *Here's to minerals!*

I heard a distant man in a bar
Sing *Here's to the cosmos!*

– Lauding everything, near and far,
Near a big black hole in an ultimate bar.
(Chorus of Astrophysicists:)
> He need not have relished each particle
> And force as the genuine article,
> But he did just that. All together now –
> Here's to him – and here's to you –
> And *Here's to the cosmos,* through and through!
> Drink – drink – drink – to all of it,
> And stay away from the black black pit.

PRINTSHOP 1922: A TRUE MOMENT

The General Secretary of the Union
Turns up one Monday morning without notice,
As he prefers. The Works Manager allows him
To walk the shopfloor talking to the workers;
He could hardly, once in a while, refuse him this.

The General Secretary (quietly, but others can hear him)
Greets young Albert Whitaker with these words:
'Are you a member of my Union?'
'Yes, sir.' 'So are you proud to be?' 'Sir! – *yes*.'
'Then you'll wear a clean collar and tie at your machine.'

FACILITATOR

He loosens the clip and shifts the microphone up
To the mouth of the Mover of the Resolution.
Then he's up again to coax it back down to where
It meets the lips of the shorter Seconder.
He's out from a chair in the wings every time,
For the nervous or the furious, for the emollient
With their cargo of delicate adverbs.

Were he not there, they couldn't make themselves heard
Without crouching, or craning upwards. And when
'It's your turn now' he lifts the head from its stand,
Softly tapping it as he strides out obligingly
To give it to every Chair-approved supporter
Wanting to take it; and grabs it back again:
He knows the power they feel with the microphone,

He knows the powerlessness of the power they feel,
The amplification of hopes not to be fulfilled,
The booming recollections of past successes
That should offer them inspiration for today . . .
Before there were microphones they had to shout
To be heard by each other in the wilderness.
Now they can shout, in the wilderness, louder still.

MR BANISTER

Our chemistry master, Mr Banister
(Not his real name) had only the one arm.
When the test tube cracked in the roarious flame
Of the bunsen burner, he replaced it four times
One winter afternoon. At the fifth attempt
Things went well enough for him to turn to the board
And with the one hand write up the formula
For his modest success.
                Sometimes
He was slow up the stairs and we sat more quietly
Than at other times fearing his fury,
If he heard any noise as he turned the corner,
And limped along the top floor corridor
To growl his way into the lab that still
Returns in dreams (and why?)
                Mr Banister
Hated teaching us, I think. 'Get *on* with something'
Was the phrase he used when he didn't want
To teach us anything at all, and sat on the stool
Behind the bunsen burner, the sink, the tap,
And in front of an empty board, as the light failed
Reading Simenon, the first time I'd ever heard
Of this author, whom I took to be a chemist.
The book he held in his hand was called *Lost Moorings.*

A DESELECTION
(i.m. Ion Jogaru, masseur)

He knew through his blindness where to touch the pain,
And hammer until it eased out and slipped away
In the morning sunlight. He thumped at speed, up and down,
On the drum of the clenched back, and the strains relaxed.
He pressed his sinuous oils into muscles and bones
And the whole day loosened and lightened.

He played games of chess, by touch and memory,
With the gym instructor, on a board beside his couch,
And did lose sometimes. A week before he died,
He bewailed with anger the performance of
Their soccer team, which had failed to qualify.
With the help of the Sports page and a dictionary,

I said, 'Had they made it, the commentators
In the BBC box would have had a merry time
With the name of the striker, Ciudea-Munteanescu'
– The wrong name to mention . . . His huge healing hands
Came down like a Carpathian rockfall on my shoulders.
'The Devil take them for deselecting him!'

THE MALICE OF COINCIDENCE

The head of the woman seen in the jacuzzi
Two years ago, an unforgettable head
As her fingers threaded the water to and fro,
An almost Gorgon head, the hair like Medusa's,
Turns up above the neck of the brand-named uniform
Of a private paramedic . . .
                              He had said to the dog No, *No!*
Bu the dog sprang, and in the corridor of the Unit
A madman – or a happy man – is singing,
With hefty forearms urging himself ever forward
Into the courtyard sunshine past the machine
Announcing *Coffee* but placarded OUT OF ORDER.
And would this woman remember his staring too long
As he passed the rippling jacuzzi on his way back
From the scented sauna to the Reception where
You paid for the facilities later?
He himself recalled the black censorious eyes
Accusing him that afternoon. 'You *look* too much!
You erode my dignity as a healthCare consultant
Proud to work for the capital "C" in the company name.'
– Who now, under the doctor's supervision,
Administers the first of several daily
Rabies injections to this forgotten starer.
What the man in the wheelchair sings is not relevant,
But I'll quote the unlucky first line of it,
An unfortunate ditty: 'I dreamt I dwelt
In marble halls' – if I heard him correctly.

THE CASE AGAINST CANUTE

When jeans became the insolence of the rich
We returned on principle to three-piece suits,
In the style of Clement Attlee and Stafford Cripps . . .
But dissidence is an ambiguous affair:
In not conforming we needed to be aware
That to go against the trend was a tactic which
Also characterised the cunning three-line whips
Of Alternative Modishness, who were equally in cahoots

With Money. 'Whatever it is, I'm against it!'
Was a dictum of the philosopher Marx, Groucho
– And it worked if it grabbed attention and rang the till.
The idea was, Don't just stay there in the swim,
Devise some ingenious utterly dissim-
ilar food – or scent – or therapy for complaints it
Was stylish to have, and in *that* way fulfil
The requirements of high fashion's in-and-out show.

Best of all at this was the legendary king
Whom we see as the sad victim of his rotten
Pride and self-delusion. In reality,
He'd fired the consultants who told him he should abide
By their focus-group researches of the tide,
And became immortal by staking everything
On a subtle scheme to go down in history
As the ultimate dissident. Mad, yes – but not forgotten.

POEM FOR THE OLDER PERSON
(*for Peter Porter*)

With an indrawn sigh, 'Why is "sex" going on so long?
The columns, the pictures, the girl's song

Rock "critics" say is "her sexiest so far"?
It should have finished long ago, but my car

Radio (on the wrong channel) goes on yammering
About it as if sex were *new*. It's hammering

Home outdated points which the world must have learnt
Fifty years ago. Yes?'
                    I draw up, having earnt

A cautious drink with this grumbling, at a place
(If you *must* know) just off the A12 . . . I present a face

That contrives an effortful smile at a barman
Who will certainly strive to serve me, when he can,

He promises as much – but he's sorry, he has to see
To the crowd that's just come in. They're ferociously

Fond of each other, they're shabby, rich, and rowdy
(Please pity this underpaid barman . . . it's a crowd he

Knows well, they've come Friday night for the last
Six weeks in their 4 by 4's . . . But the fad won't last)

And they talk sex, sex, sex as they order drinks
– While this bubble in the corner floats and 'thinks'

'Why is "sex" going on so [fucking] long?'

NEW YEAR

It was all about taking my first
Breaths of every New Year from the sea,
In the dark, in the cold, by myself;
Then to walk on planning to leave
A long trail of prints which a tide
Would erase by dawn . . .
Except that a light in the dunes
– Then a whole whistling spray of lights –
Ruled out my solitude.
When I spoke to those two I confessed
My secret vow, and they wished
Me happiness, as you would,
Then said, 'Stay, if you wish!' But I turned
Away with excuses, the cold,
There were friends I should meet, I was tired,
And none of it true.
                              It would come
After less than ten yards, my regret
At the resolution I'd kept.

THE ARROWS

They point in a line across the foot of the page
To a kiss that ends the letter in the farthest
Right-hand corner.

Most of the arrows believe, 'She will see the kiss
Without our help, why should we all line up
To take our turn at pointing out the kiss?

'We could refer to another place or object,
Directions for someone actually *unsure*
About where he is going.'

But the wisest of the arrows addresses
The rest of them saying, 'If we took off our heads
And straightened them, and crossed them with our bodies

We could one by one become kisses ourselves in turn,
And the thousands more in the queue off the left-hand edge
Would know they have something to wait for.

DECEMBER 31ST 2009

I step down in dying light
From the table on which I stood
On this last day of a decade
Screwing in a low energy bulb,
A token of somebody's scheme
For empowering me to be good,
And to play my part in small ways.
But the online newscasts reveal
Hour by hour how the larger thieves
Go on playing a different game
To pollute and cloud over our days.

The nought years have gone to their end
Like supplements gladly thrown in
With spent bottles and cartons and cans
To a good Green Citizen's bin.
The media historians
Will recount to us how we all lived,
The garments Celebrity wore,
The musics we should have preferred,
And which reputations survived
An acclaim they did not deserve.
But we already know the score.

When the bulb has brightened, I read
In hard-copy broadsheets of wars
That extended and raged unresolved,
Of treaties saluting the need
For the brokers of power to stay rich.
Through these last ten years famine gripped
Regions out of humanity's reach.
The measures we could have applied

To plant hope in a field of defeats
Went ignored, were the drowned-out song
Of long marches down monitored streets.

However you try, it's a task
To retrieve fast-vanishing fact
From among coloured spreads which maintain
'All you want is our visual world,
We permit you to see but not learn,
And not think – and above all, not act.'
In ingenious graphics, a dance
Of computerised death fills the screens
Where the language of management rules,
Cloaked in mantras which conceal
The crimes of its ignorance.

Though my writing's a hapless scrawl
Compared with four decades ago,
It might serve to cite one surprise
From the final hours of this year:
In a train stopped by seasonal snow
On a Circle Line platform, all eyes
Leaving tabloid headlines to fall
On the middle of nowhere, most hands
Clamped on cellphones, this occurred:
Something moved in front of our feet
Where we sat in dull silence – a bird.

Through doors open wide to the air
Where we'd halted at Edgware Road
(Perhaps to find out where we were)
The creature hopped in and patrolled

Past our bags as it foraged for crumbs.
Then the voice called, 'Doors closing, the train
Is about to depart.' All it had
Was its grey urban wings, to fly out
At around waist level and scare
Waiting 'customers' – landing again
Near a flickering platform ad.

It was not out to symbolise
The shortness of all our lives
With this three minutes exercise,
It just took its liberty
Of renouncing our heedless faces,
Getting out while the going was good,
Not desiring to stay on and be
Conveyed to too many more places
Where you clicked on Democracy
To find Freedom was a strict law
And Choice was compulsory.

Knowing what it was all about,
It appeared to forsake the entire
Shebang of our twenty-first
Century of terror and doubt.
– And its call was important to us.
There were wisdoms we might acquire
From its take on our decade's events:
When such powerful evils desire
To target us with their own aims,
Could we not ourselves form a flock
Migrating to common sense?

Are the limits of reason reached, where
Affirmation may only be said
To exist in football chants,
In New Year sieges of stores,
In flagged-up parades of the dead?
Has each truly affirmative cause
Become a mere shrug of despair?
I am sorry to fear, now it's dark,
That only the worst lies ahead;
Though the least we could show from now on
Is an odd affirmative spark.